AF131487

BOOK ANALYSIS

Written by Natacha Cerf and Célia Ramain
Translated by Emma Hanna

A Dry White Season

Season
BY ANDRÉ BRINK

ANDRÉ BRINK

SOUTH AFRICAN WRITER

- **Born in Vrede (South Africa) in 1935.**
- **Died on a flight from the Netherlands to South Africa in 2015.**
- **Notable works:**
  - *Looking on Darkness* (1973), novel
  - *The Blue Door* (2006), novel
  - *A Fork in the Road* (2009), memoir

André Brink was a teacher, novelist, playwright, essayist and committed anti-apartheid activist. He was born into a middle-class Afrikaner family, meaning that he was a direct descendent of the earliest Dutch colonists to arrive in South Africa, and was raised in an environment that was built on the racist and nationalist beliefs that he would later spend his life fighting against through his writing.

After spending a number of years at university in South Africa, he travelled to Paris in 1959 to study comparative literature at the Sorbonne

University. His time there opened his eyes to the senselessness of segregation and racial discrimination, and he went on to create a body of literary work, written in both Afrikaans (a Germanic language native to South Africa) and English, which is closely connected to his homeland's political history.

Brink died just days after being awarded an honorary doctorate from the Université catholique de Louvain (Belgium) while on the return flight to Cape Town.

A DRY WHITE SEASON

AN ENDLESS STRUGGLE

- **Genre:** novel
- **Reference edition:** Brink, A. (1984) *A Dry White Season*. London: Penguin.
- **1ˢᵗ edition:** 1979
- **Themes:** South Africa, apartheid, justice, equality, struggle, racism

A Dry White Season is André Brink's fourth novel, and brought him to worldwide renown. It was published in South Africa in 1979, but was immediately banned by the authorities. However, it was then republished by a London-based publishing house, which led to the book being translated into multiple languages and winning France's Prix Médicis étranger in 1980.

The novel is set in Johannesburg in 1976, and tells the story of an Afrikaner teacher named Ben Du Toit. One of his students, Jonathan, participates in the Soweto uprising to protest the promotion of Afrikaans as an official language in schools, and is arrested by the Special Branch, as is his father Gordon. They are both tortured and killed during their detention, and Ben decides to attempt to uncover the truth of the matter so that the perpetrators can be brought to justice. However, this decision comes at a heavy price...

SUMMARY

A WORRYING DISAPPEARANCE

In June 1976, Jonathan, the son of the black cleaner who works at the school where Ben Du Toit teaches, takes part in the Soweto uprising, and is never seen or heard from again. His parents, Gordon and Emily Ngubene, are unable to get any information from the police, so with Ben's help they hire a lawyer called Dan Levinson. The special police tell Levinson that Jonathan was killed during the uprising, and that his unidentified body was buried a month ago.

Gordon investigates further and discovers that his son was arrested and tortured by the Special Branch, which wanted to use him as a scapegoat for the riots. Gordon wants justice for his son, and convinces the witnesses to make a statement; however, he is arrested the following day. Ben goes to see Colonel Viljoen in an attempt to find out why Gordon was arrested, but his efforts are in vain.

Gordon's clothing is returned to Emily, who finds traces of dried blood and three broken teeth in the material. Another man who was detained at the same time as Gordon says that when he saw him, Gordon was unable to walk or talk properly, and that his face seemed to be swollen as a result of multiple beatings.

Gordon's lawyer manages to gather enough eyewitness accounts to build a viable case, but at the hearing, the witnesses who testify on behalf of the Special Branch persuade the judge not to give a final verdict. A fortnight later, the news breaks that Gordon is dead.

A SUSPICIOUS DEATH

Ben goes to a predominantly black neighbourhood to examine Gordon's body, accompanied by Stanley, a friend of the Ngubenes. Although Gordon's corpse is dressed in fine clothes, when Ben examines the body itself, he discovers that it is emaciated and covered in poorly disguised wounds.

During the investigation, all the evidence that Gordon was tortured to death is judged to be unfounded and insufficient. His death is therefore ruled to have been a suicide by hanging, and all claims that it was caused by negligence or mistreatment are dismissed. At the end of the hearing, Ben meets a journalist called Melanie Bruwer, while an officer from the Special Branch called Stolz searches his home and confiscates his notes about the start of his private investigation, as well as some letters and personal journals.

Ben wants to gather enough evidence to have the case reopened, so Emily gives him two brief letters that Gordon wrote to her during his imprisonment, one on a scrap of lined paper and one on a square of toilet paper. Although the first message does not openly say that he is being mistreated, the second leaves no room for doubt:

> *"My dear wife I am still in these conditions* (followed by a few illegible words) *worse and too much pain you must try to help me for they do not want to* (illegible) *me. You must care for the children and if you need money you must ask the church or my* (illegible) *master who is kind to us. I do not know if I will come home alive because they are very* (illegible) *but God will provide and I miss you very much. Try to help me because..."* (p. 176)

From that point on, Ben focuses his efforts on finding the individuals involved in order to try to persuade them to make further statements. He is particularly eager to get a statement from the doctor who performed the autopsy, although this proves difficult, as the doctor is afraid of the reprisals he could face if he speaks out. These fears prove to be justified the very next day, when he and his family are placed under house arrest for five years.

A BATTLE WITH GRAVE CONSEQUENCES

Ben's efforts have numerous consequences: he is placed under heavy surveillance, meaning that his telephone is bugged by the police, his mail is intercepted and his friends and colleagues are questioned about him. In addition, the Communist symbol is painted on his door, his tyres are slashed, his son is bullied at school, and many black people who have suffered oppression and have heard about Ben's efforts to secure justice for Gordon come to his house asking for help. This endless stream of beggars soon takes a heavy toll on his personal life and his mental health, but he is unable to turn them away.

Most of the witnesses who agree to sign a statement are arrested by the Special Branch shortly afterwards. Ben is consumed by regret, as many of the people he identified during his investigation have been exiled, jailed or even murdered. Emily throws herself in front of a train after learning that her other son, Robert, has been killed by a patrol from the South African army while trying to cross the border into Mozambique. Meanwhile, Melanie, who has started an affair with Ben, loses her South African citizenship, meaning that her right of residence in the country is revoked.

Ben talks to Colonel Viljoen about the intimidation tactics used by the Special Branch, but this only exacerbates the situation: that night, someone in the street shoots at his house. He notifies the press, but the editor of the Afrikaans-language newspaper deems the story too dangerous to publish. Ben therefore approaches an English-language newspaper instead, even as he starts to lose all hope in his cause. The article sends shockwaves rippling across the country, but consequences soon follow: the newspaper is sued for libel, and the reporter is sentenced to a year in prison for refusing to name his sources.

Meanwhile, the lawyer Dan Levinson flees the country and is granted political asylum in London, where he organises several conferences on police brutality in South Africa. However, it is revealed that he also swindled many of his black clients by setting exorbitant prices and demanding fees that they had already paid.

ENDLESS SOLITUDE

Ben feels utterly powerless and no longer knows who to turn to. He resigns from his job, and his wife, Susan, decides to leave him shortly afterwards, as she has been subjected to the intimidation tactics used by the Special Branch and has also discovered her husband's affair. Ben is left with no one supporting him except his son Johan, who is the last member of his family to openly stand by him. He then goes to visit Stanley in Soweto, but Stanley's wife informs him that he has fled to Botswana.

Ben's daughter, Suzette, with whom he has always had a strained relationship, suddenly starts acting unusually caring and attentive towards him. During one of their conversations, Ben tells her where he has hidden his documents about the investigation. However, when he returns home, he is gripped by the sudden fear that the reason for Suzette's sudden kindness is that she is actually acting as a police informant, and takes the precaution of moving all his papers. The following night, someone breaks into his garage and searches through the toolbox where all of his documents had previously been hidden. Knowing that his daughter has betrayed him, Ben concocts a ruse and innocently asks her to keep all the papers for him. He is hoping to use this subterfuge to trick the authorities and divert their attention, allowing him to post his real notes about the investigation to a journalist.

Shortly afterwards, Ben is hit by a car and killed. A week later, his friend receives the package and decides to publish the report, in spite of the risks this entails, "[s]o that it will not be possible for any man ever to say again: I knew nothing about it" (p. 316).

CHARACTER STUDY

BEN DU TOIT

Ben Du Toit is a 52-year-old history and geography teacher of Afrikaner descent. He leads an orderly life which revolves around his family, his job and his love of DIY. He and his wife Susan have three children: Suzette, Linda and Johan.

When Jonathan, the son of the cleaner of the school Ben works at, goes missing and then dies in suspicious circumstances, Ben's life is thrown into chaos. He is the only Afrikaner (and therefore the only white man) who has ever treated Jonathan's father Gordon kindly: specifically, when some money was stolen from one of the school's classrooms, the other teachers were quick to point the finger at Gordon, but Ben defended him against these false accusations, and discovered that some of the final-year students were the real culprits after investigating the incident. Later, when he found out that Jonathan was intending to leave school due to lack of funds, despite being a brilliant student,

Ben offered to pay for his studies out of his own pocket. Gordon therefore comes to Ben for help.

Through his friendship with Gordon, Ben gradually becomes familiar with the conditions that black people are forced to live in under the apartheid regime. When Gordon also disappears and is killed in suspicious circumstances, Ben decides to pursue the matter and keep fighting for the truth. He wins over a number of supporters (such as Melanie Bruwer and Stanley), but the opposition he faces is much stronger, and his fight against the government's lies brings him into direct conflict with the powerful Special Branch. Ben is left isolated, overwhelmed and devastated by the deaths that are piling up around him, and starts doubting everything he has done: "How much longer must the list grow of those who pay the price of my efforts to clear Gordon's name?" (p. 267). When faced with very real danger, Ben displays great bravery and commitment, and ensures that his work outlives him by passing his notes on to one of his former classmates, who is now a writer.

GORDON NGUBENE

Gordon works as a cleaner at the school where Ben Du Toit teaches. He is married to Emily and is Jonathan's father, and is a good husband, a good father and a fair, likeable man who never does any harm to anyone.

In addition to his job as a cleaner, Gordon and his family also do odd jobs for the Du Toit family as thanks for Ben's support when he was accused of theft.

Gordon is from Transkei (former Bantustan in South Africa, 1976-1994), and was a gifted student who managed to complete his secondary education despite his academic career being interrupted by family problems on multiple occasions. Although he cares more about his life in the city than his roots in Transkei, he nevertheless sends his eldest son Jonathan back to his homeland so that he can be "circumcised and initiated" (p. 38).

He is left in a state of shock when his son is killed in suspicious circumstances following the Soweto uprising, and his desire to give Jonathan a proper burial and his sense of honour and justice spur him to attempt to discover the truth about his death. He takes countless risks during his quest for the truth, displaying great courage and determination. He is eventually arrested by the Special Branch and dies under torture, just like his son.

EMILY NGUBENE

Emily is Gordon's wife, and they have two sons, Jonathan and Robert. She lives in a house built from cement and corrugated iron in a low-income area in Soweto, and is a generous, caring, well-organised mother. She always treats Ben respectfully, even though many of the black people in her neighbourhood are wary of him because he is white, and even seek to harm him.

When Gordon is imprisoned, Emily displays great composure, bravery and determination, but she is plunged into utter despair when he is killed: she loses all her previous optimism, and becomes convinced that justice will never be done. The death of her younger son Robert saps her of her remaining strength and drives her to commit suicide.

SUSAN DU TOIT

Susan is Ben's wife, and the mother of Suzette, Linda and Johan. She initially seems like the epitome of middle-class politeness, propriety and respectability, but the good manners that she is expected to display at all times secretly weigh on her, and she often reproaches her husband and addresses him sarcastically. She believes that he is a failure and that he is responsible for what she sees as their unsatisfying lifestyle. They find it difficult to understand each other, and Susan does not take any interest in his chosen cause, as she selfishly places greater importance on the comforts offered by her middle-class life than having compassion for others. During Ben's fight against apartheid, Susan begins struggling with depression, and she eventually leaves him when she discovers that he has been having an affair.

SUZETTE

Suzette is the daughter of Susan and Ben Du Toit, and works as an architect in Pretoria. She resembles her mother in terms of both physical appearance and personality, as she is tall with blonde hair, blue eyes and a similar physique and has a forthright, extroverted personality. She is highly career-driven, and spends very little time with her son as a result; she also has a poor relationship with his father, whom she tends to scold and mock frequently. When Susan leaves Ben, Suzette is unusually kind and helpful to him, but it is soon revealed that she has an ulterior motive for doing so: she is collaborating with the Special Branch, and is simply trying to get close to him so that she can betray him more easily.

STANLEY MAKHAYA

Stanley is a friend of the Ngubene family, and works as an unregistered taxi driver. This job has allowed him to build up an extensive network of contacts who keep him informed of all the latest goings-on. He is described as a "corpulent man, over six feet tall, with an enormous belly and the neck of a bull, and several double chins [...] Very black. With light palms" (p. 53). Stanley is initially very wary of Ben and openly mocks him by calling him "lanie" (which means "white man" in Bantu, the family of languages spoken throughout southern Africa). Ben's ignorance about the conditions black people have to live in frequently irritates him: "'You're white.' As if that summarised everything. 'Hope comes easy to you. You're used to it.'" (p. 83). However, he and Ben eventually become friends after discovering that they had similar childhoods and through their mutual support for Gordon.

MELANIE BRUWER

Melanie is a reporter for the *Mail*, and has dual British and South African citizenship. Ben is immediately attracted to her: "her youth had struck him as almost vulnerable, an openness, a frankness, a freshness [...] an affirmation, un-nerving in its force, of unflinching womanness" (p. 115).

Melanie provides Ben with unwavering support, which is all the more remarkable given that very few other white people are prepared to stand in solidarity with South Africa's black population. However, this can be explained by her position as a kind of outsider (through her dual British and South African citizenship), which gives her a more detached, critical perspective on South Africa's white Afrikaner population, since it is not the only community she belongs to. She has also inherited a great deal of her father's militant resolve.

Ben and Melanie's relationship eventually turns romantic in nature, which is the final nail in the coffin for Ben's marriage after Susan receives a photograph of the two of them unmistakably locked in an embrace. The photograph was presumably sent by the Special Branch, which also prevents Melanie from returning to South Africa by stripping her of her citizenship and right of residence.

PHIL BRUWER

Phil is Melanie's father, and is a surly, impolite, colourful individual. However, he is also very wise, as reflected by his job as a philosophy teacher, and the views he expresses show that he is highly educated. He moved to Germany to study philosophy in the 1930s, but returned to South Africa when Hitler (German dictator, 1889-1945) rose to power. He then went back to fight against the Nazis when World War II (1939-1945) was declared, and spent three years in a prisoner-of-war camp.

His physical appearance is described briefly: "Small goatee stained with tobacco juice. The skin of his face dark and tanned like old leather, like an old discarded shoe; and two twinkling dark brown eyes half-disappearing below the unkempt eyebrows" (pp. 185-186).

STOLZ

Captain Stolz is one of the leaders of the Special Branch, and is the embodiment of everything Ben is fighting against: corruption, violence, hatred, and so on. He is described as tall and thin, with "[s]trangely dark eyes for such a pale face. The thin white line of a scar on his cheek" (p. 60). His attitude immediately makes Ben uneasy:

> "[H]e leans against the wall, playing with an orange which he throws up and catches, and throws up and catches monotonously; and every time it lands in his white hand he pauses momentarily to squeeze it briefly, voluptuously, his gaze unflinching on your face. He remains uncomfortably out of sight behind your back when you sit down on the chair the colonel has offered you." (p. 58)

He has orchestrated the "disappearance" of many black people, disguising their deaths as suicides. He also threatens Ben one final time before he is murdered:

> "Stolz didn't move in his chair.
> 'Now don't rush things. I'm offering you a chance.'
> 'You mean my very last chance?'
> 'One never knows.'" (p. 281)

The fact that "Stolz" is a German-sounding name leads the reader to associate the segregationist regime in South Africa with the racist Nazi regime. Furthermore, Melanie's father explicitly compares the two regimes:

> "It's all System and no God. Sooner or later people start believing in their way of life as an absolute: immutable, fundamental, a precondition. Saw it with my own eyes in Germany in the Thirties. A whole nation running after the Idea, like Gadarene swine. *Sieg heil, sieg heil*. Keeps me awake at night. [...] And now I see it happening in my own country, step by step. Terrifyingly predictable." (p. 187)

ANALYSIS

THE HISTORICAL CONTEXT

The colonisation of South Africa

In 1652, Dutch settlers founded a colony in present-day Cape Town. They were soon followed by more colonisers from a variety of other European countries, including Germany, Scandinavia and France (specifically French Protestants, known as Huguenots, who fled the country en masse after the Edict of Nantes, which made it legal to practise Protestantism in France, was revoked in 1685). This early influx of colonisers marked the start of slavery in South Africa.

These early colonisers came to be known as "Boers" (which is Dutch for "farmer"), because the majority of them made a living through agriculture and raising livestock. In more recent years, it has become more common to refer to this community of white Protestants, whose native language is an offshoot of Dutch known as Afrikaans, as "Afrikaners".

After the Congress of Vienna, which was held in 1814 in order to re-establish European borders following the fall of Napoleon (French emperor, 1769-1821), the Cape Town colony became British territory, English became its official language and slavery was abolished in 1833. This resulted in the emergence of strong nationalist sentiment among the Boers, who were opposed to cultural assimilation and believed that the new British policies were too favourable to the black population. This culminated in the Boer population migrating to the country's interior in what is known as the Great Trek (1834-1839), which the Boers viewed as a quasi-Biblical exodus, leading the community to begin seeing themselves as a "chosen" people who were superior to others.

The Boers clashed with the British on a number of occasions before eventually becoming a political power in their own right and establishing a presence within the country's government. As a result, a policy of racial segregation was established in 1921, after initially being proposed in 1913. From that point on, a growing number of increasingly discriminatory and racist measures were approved by the authorities each year, the Boers having successfully wrested power out of British hands. They had three primary goals:

- to reverse all prior cultural and social progress;
- to introduce a new religious ideology based on racial superiority;
- to protect the Boer identity from the "threat" posed by the black population.

Apartheid

Apartheid (which means "separation" in Afrikaans) is the most common name for the regime which enforced the systematic racial segregation of the population of South Africa between 1948 and 1991, although measures which acted as precursors to the official apartheid regime were put forward by the government from as early as 1913. The measures imposed during this period included:

- the prohibition of mixed-race marriages;
- the prohibition of sexual relations between white and non-white individuals;
- the prohibition of Communist political parties;
- the classification of individuals according to

race;

- the division of urban residential areas according to race;
- the requirement that black individuals carry a valid pass book in order to enter certain zones of the country;
- the revocation of black workers' right to strike;
- the revocation of black individuals' right to receive professional training;
- the racial segregation of many public amenities such as toilets and drinking fountains;
- the racial segregation of all official and public places (schools, offices, hospitals, restaurants, cinemas, parks, etc.).

In 1960, a protest against the internal passport system was so brutally repressed that it came to be known as the Sharpeville massacre. Despite the introduction of a series of increasingly oppressive measures, black resistance also began gaining traction, led by Nelson Mandela (South African lawyer and politician, 1918-2013), who was sentenced to life imprisonment in 1964. Following a political struggle led by democratic African political parties, which were supported by the international community, apartheid was finally abolished in 1991. On 10 May 1994, Mandela became the first black president of South Africa.

It is clear that *A Dry White Season* was written and is set in this political and historical context. For example, the protagonist's surname, Du Toit, could be a reference to the historical figure Stephanus Jacobus du Toit (1847-1911), who founded the Afrikaner Bond (which means "Afrikaner League" in Afrikaans) in 1879 with the aim of promoting the Afrikaans language as a symbol of Afrikaner nationalism. This gives Ben Du Toit a connection to the entire colonial history of South Africa, as he is a descendent of French colonists and also seems to have family connections to an Afrikaner nationalist.

A NOVEL IN STEP WITH CURRENT EVENTS

André Brink first travelled to France in 1959 to enrol at the Sorbonne University, and he studied there until 1961. His time in France made him realise how unjust the apartheid system was, as the black students he met at university were considered equal to the white students. This was when Brink discovered his literary vocation: to denounce the horrors of institutionalised racism through literature and thus help improve the political, social and moral situation of his country.

Brink began writing *A Dry White Season* a year before the death of Steve Biko (South African activist, 1946-1977), who was one of the leading figures of the fight against apartheid and who was arrested, tortured and killed by the police in 1977, while Mandela was imprisoned on Robben Island. Brink temporarily stopped writing *A Dry White Season* as a result of these events, and only completed the novel at a later date.

The novel's depiction of life in South Africa in the 1970s is entirely realistic, although the story itself is fictional. Literature gives writers a means of transcending the transient nature of political conflicts to immortalise their own philosophical reflections and perspectives on human relationships in eloquent prose that can stand the test of time. While journalism often merely scratches the surface of the issues surrounding an event or a series of events, and chiefly focuses on the facts and the sequence of events, literature explores the deeper forces of human nature that influence these events, which in this case are primarily related to society. Furthermore, *A Dry White Season* is a work of notable historical significance, as it contributed to the efforts of many writers and artists to raise awareness of the situation in South Africa in democratic countries in Europe and America, which then placed increasing pressure on the South African government to establish a democracy in which all citizens would be treated equally. The worldwide attention that Brink's novel received (including prestigious prizes such as the Martin Luther King Memorial Prize for the English version and the Prix Médicis étranger for the French translation) allowed his outrage to be heard by a wider audience, and undeniably helped to create a place for black South Africans at the negotiating table.

TWO SEPARATE WORLDS

The fundamental division of South African society at this time lies at the heart of the novel. Brink uses fiction to explore the issue of multiculturalism, meaning the coexistence of multiple cultures which are prone to clashing, and each of which is wholly independent, with its own traditions and perception of the other. This means that the greatest challenge for the author is to create a vivid, well-developed portrayal of each of these cultures, while also exploring the possible connections between them.

Brink primarily concentrates on depicting white society in the novel, meaning the districts, political structures, schools, leisure pursuits and familial activities that delineate white people's daily lives. Brink also shows how their world is upheld by a totalitarian legal system which justifies racist propaganda, violence and abuses.

However, the author takes equal care when portraying the world inhabited by black South Africans. Although they represent the majority of the population, the oppression they face on a daily basis means that they are forced to live in townships such as Soweto or other squalid ghettoes where they are sent to form a reserve workforce. However, the seeds of rebellion have taken root in the hearts of young people across the country, who are no longer prepared to tolerate the unfair laws that give white people utter supremacy over them with the complicity of the country's legal, religious, administrative, educational and social institutions.

However, Brink's goal is not to reduce South African society to a simple dichotomy of black versus white, with no room for nuance: in *A Dry White Season*, each of these communities is also divided against itself. In other words, the rifts that divide the country reflect the variety of different languages and environments that can be found within it, such as the traditional farms in rural areas, the large cities and the suburbs. In particular, many social classes coexist in the suburbs, meaning that a tremendous variety of people live there, each with their own ways of reacting to oppression. This is equally true of white society, where those of British descent constantly clash with the Afrikaner community. For example, while the Afrikaans-language press refuses to support Ben's cause, the English-language press does not hesitate to publish reports on legal scandals and police brutality.

However, some people attempt to forge connections and alliances across these divides, including the protagonist Ben Du Toit, who embarks on a determined quest to secure justice for Gordon and Jonathan. His search for the truth estranges him from those around him: he is misunderstood and rejected by his family, friends and colleagues, none of whom understand why he is so invested in helping people whom they do not even see as fully human.

However, he also faces rejection from another, arguably more significant source: namely, the black community that he is trying to help, who are mistrustful of his intentions and insult and threaten him. This means that in his attempt to act in solidarity with the black community, Ben not only estranges himself from the racism of white society, but is also unable to join a new community. This is arguably because his desire to act as a "white saviour" is itself an act of oppression born of white paternalism, leaving him unable to bypass the barrier between him and the black community.

In fact, this is perhaps the main political issue addressed in the novel, as Ben's good intentions are not enough to counterbalance his ignorance, and he frequently falls into the role of the oppressor. For example, Emily's nickname for him, "Baas", is extremely telling, as it means "master" in Afrikaans. Furthermore, the fact that Ben does not know the Bantu vocabulary Stanley uses, and above all the fact that he assumes that Stanley is Xhosa (a Bantu ethnic group from Southern Africa) like Gordon, while Stanley is actually Zulu (another Bantu ethnic group from Southern Africa), illustrates his ignorance about this disparate community.

As a result, Ben is doomed to linger in an inherently hostile liminal space between these two worlds, which ultimately leads to his death. In the final pages of the book, the absurdity of his chosen role as a hero who has been rejected by those he is trying to defend is made even clearer:

> "All I did was to turn the window down an inch or so to shout at them: "Don't you understand? I'm on your side!" My voice breaking with hysteria. Then the first stone hit the body of the car." (p. 302)

Having been abandoned and betrayed by his family and his peers, and distrusted and threatened by the black community, Ben's situation is perhaps best summed up by Stanley's comment:

"Forget it, you're a foreigner" (p. 168).

THE THEME OF SOLITUDE

Brink's work betrays a certain fascination with solitude and the difficulty of forging meaningful bonds with others. While the struggle for justice in South Africa is central to most of his work, other major recurring themes include human relationships and the feelings that bind one person to another. Brink cited the French writer Albert Camus (1913-1960) as one of his chief literary influences, particularly his character Meursault, the protagonist of *The Outsider* (1942).

Brink's affinity with Camus's writing could also be explained by the latter's exploration of the relationship between the words "solitude" and "solidarity", notably in his 1951 essay *The Rebel*, which directly addresses the link between personal rebellion, which is the act of opposing injustice on an individual level, and collective action to counter unfairness and oppression.

Brink's choice of literature as a vehicle for attempting to raise awareness about the unjust fate of the colonised people of South Africa places him firmly in the literary tradition established by Camus. He made no secret of his admiration for the philosopher of rebellion and the Absurd, and even translated his novel *The Plague* (1947) into Afrikaans. Brink discussed his debt to Camus in his autobiography *A Fork in the Road* (2009):

> "And then there was Camus. Who promptly became, and still is, one of the Baudelairean *phares* of my life. I do not merely admire Camus, I love him." (Brink, 2009: 132-133)

Brink's admiration and love for Camus are also made clear in *A Dry White Season* through an explicit reference:

> "One always has a choice. Don't fool yourself. Only be thankful you made the choice you did. Not an original thought, I admit. Camus. But one can do worse than listening to him." (p. 190)

HISTORICAL AND LITERARY AMBITION

One of the principle characteristics of *A Dry White Season* is the way it uses literary language to narrate a historical account of injustice.

Brink imbues the story with a certain degree of objectivity by using a nested narrative, meaning that although Ben is the protagonist of the story, he is not its primary narrator: instead, that role goes to his old friend, who writes love stories and adventure novels.

For the most part, Ben is simply a character in the story that is being told, but he does occasionally narrate portions of the story in the first person, for example through extracts of his journal: "25 February. I'm making fewer and fewer notes" (p. 266).

This dual narration can be explained by Brink's desire to create some distance between him and the story. In an almost anachronistic way, Ben could be considered a whistleblower, as a single event propels him to embark on investigation, which comprises forensic reports, witness statements and other documents, and the evidence he amasses eventually allows him to formulate a critical viewpoint with the aim of raising awareness about the injustice it documents. Ben is ostracised as a result, and Brink shared a similar fate, as his novel was banned by the South African authorities as soon as it was published in 1979.

However, *A Dry White Season* cannot be described as a purely objective testimonial, as Brink's command of language throughout the novel is remarkable. In addition to the use of clever stylistic devices such as the frame story, the characters are drawn in rich, vibrant detail and their emotions are constantly made clear to the reader through the use of a distinctive narrative style and rhythm. So, for example, Ben's (justified) paranoia is made evident by the staccato phrases he starts using in his journal: "Wednesday 11 May. Strange day. Yesterday's visit by the Special Branch. Difficult to explore on paper, but I must. Writing it out in full sentences is salutary, like breathing deeply. Will try. A frontier crossed" (p. 158).

FURTHER REFLECTION

SOME QUESTIONS TO THINK ABOUT...

- Analyse the title of the book with the help of the following quote:

  > "The single memory that has been with me all day, infinitely more real than the solid school buildings, is that distant summer when Pa and I were left with the sheep. The drought that took everything from us, leaving us alone and scorched among the white skeletons [...] And it seems to me I'm finding myself on the edge of yet another dry white season, perhaps worse than the one I knew as a child." (p. 163)

- The characters' names are significant. Explain the origins of the names Ben Du Toit and Stolz.
- How does Ben overcome his own ignorance?
- In your opinion, why do the people that Ben wants to help not always welcome him with open arms?
- How does the author reflect on his own social position through the character of Ben?

- What political question does the story ask?
- How does the novel portray South Africa?
- What similarities are there between Brink and Albert Camus, and between their respective characters?
- Compare and contrast the book with its film adaptation.
- Do you know of any other works which played a role in the history of emancipation? Or of any other South African authors who took a similar approach to Brink?

We want to hear from you!
Leave a comment on your online library
and share your favourite books on social media!

FURTHER READING

REFERENCE EDITION

- Brink, A. (1984) *A Dry White Season*. London: Penguin.

REFERENCE STUDIES

- (No date) André Philippus Brink. *Larousse*. [Online]. [Accessed 23 May 2018]. Available from: <http://www.larousse.fr/encyclopedie/personnage/Andr%C3%A9_Philippus_Brink/110236>

- (No date) Apartheid. *Larousse*. [Online]. [Accessed 23 May 2018]. Available from: <http://www.larousse.fr/encyclopedie/divers/apartheid/22047>

- Fauré, M. and Bailliot, M. (2017) *Apartheid: Racial Segregation in South Africa*. Trans. Neal, R. Brussels: Plurilingua Publishing.

- Puissant Baeyens, F. (2018) *Nelson Mandela: The Fight Against Apartheid*. Trans. Neal, R. Brussels: Plurilingua Publishing.

ADAPTATIONS

- *A Dry White Season*. (1989) [Film]. Euzhan Palcy. Dir. USA: Metro Goldwyn Mayer.

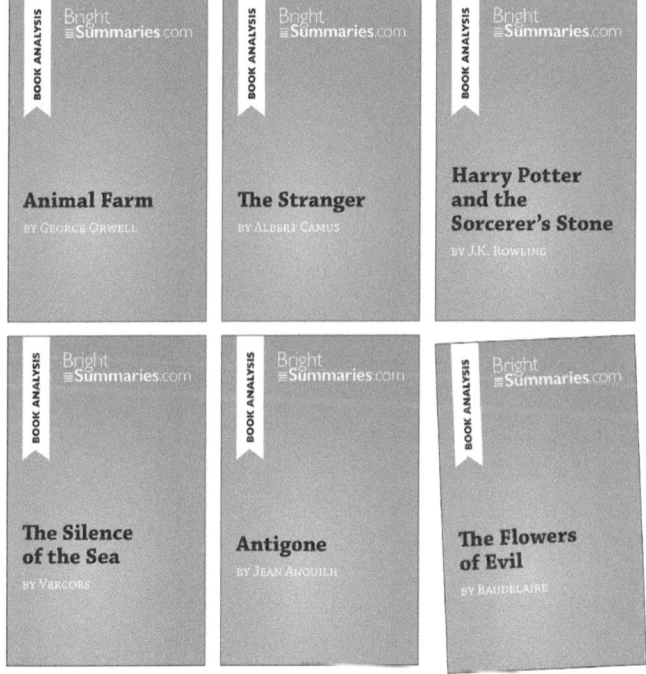

www.brightsummaries.com

Ebook EAN: 9782808010368

Paperback EAN: 9782808010375

Legal Deposit: D/2018/12603/254

This guide was written with the collaboration of Célia Ramain for the character studies of Ben Du Toit, Stanley, Melanie Bruwer, Phil Bruwer and Stolz, and the sections "The historical context" and "Historical and literary ambition".

Cover: © Primento

Digital conception by Primento, the digital partner of publishers.